D0031197

I know this to be true

NELSON MANDELA
FOUNDATION
Living the legacy

Gloria Steinem

I know this to be true

_____

on integrity,
empathy &
authenticity

Interview and photography
Geoff Blackwell

CHRONICLE BOOKS
SAN FRANCISCO

in association with

Blackwell&Ruth.

Dedicated to the legacy
and memory of
Nelson Mandela

'Ordinary people are smart, smart people are ordinary, decisions are best made by the people affected by them, and human beings have an almost infinite capacity for adapting to the expectations around us.'

Introduction

A significant portion of Gloria Steinem's life has been spent travelling. As a young child she criss-crossed America with her parents and sister living in a car and trailer. There was no plan or school, just the familiarity of the road. Survival came from money her father made selling antiques along the way.

Through this formative experience, Steinem's identity was irrevocably shaped. 'Taking to the road – by which I mean letting the road take you – changed who I thought I was,' she writes in her book *My Life on the Road*. 'The road is messy in the way that real life is messy. It leads us out of denial and into reality, out of theory and into practice, out of caution and into action, out of statistics and into stories – in short, out of our heads and into our hearts.'[1]

It also led her young heart to a belief that has stayed with her throughout her life; the conviction that all people are equal irrespective of social standing.

'Families are not about form but content. Humans are not ranked; we are linked.'[2]

In her early twenties she travelled to India, where she stayed for two years on a fellowship. There she observed Gandhian activism first-hand, discovering the traditional practice of communal talking circles where every person is equal and belongs. Where those involved learn to listen and gain an understanding of – and respect for – the views of others so that they might open their minds and hearts to connect with each other.

It proved to be a profound moment. Steinem would go on to use the technique again and again throughout her life.

Simultaneously, she was beginning to build a career as a journalist. The early seeds of this path took root upon returning to the US; she wrote pieces as a freelancer for major players including *Esquire*, *Show*, and *Cosmopolitan* magazines. In 1963 she went undercover to write an exposé on Hugh Hefner's Playboy Clubs ("A Bunny's Tale"). It garnered attention for revealing the objectification and harassment Playboy's female employees were subjected to on a daily basis. When, a few years later, her *New York* magazine article "After Black Power, Women's Liberation" was published, it established her as one of America's most prominent feminist voices.

As her career developed, the women's movement gained momentum. In 1972 she co-founded *Ms. Magazine* with child-welfare advocate Dorothy Pitman Hughes. Filling a gap that had existed for too long, *Ms.* was a new type of women's magazine both for and by women. But establishing a magazine that was staffed, financed and editorially driven by women in an industry dominated by – and accustomed to – men, was no easy feat. Despite the myriad challenges they faced, it paid off; a sample issue sold out in eight days. Within weeks, there were more than 26,000 subscription orders. Readers wanted more.

A pioneering publication, *Ms.* was the first of its kind in the US to give cover space to confronting issues such as domestic violence and sexual harassment, openly promote the Equal Rights Amendment of 1923, and feature women supporting the decriminalization of abortion. By addressing real issues, it gave women a unique platform that finally expressed their views.

As her profile grew, Steinem used her voice in a multitude of ways. She actively campaigned for a slew of issues, including women's rights – in the workplace, in the home, at educational institutions and on the street – reproductive freedom, and racial equality. Time and again she expressed the belief that all people are equal, irrespective of race, age, gender, or social standing, and should be considered as such. 'Ordinary people are smart, smart people are ordinary, decisions are best made by the people affected by them, and human beings have an almost infinite capacity for adapting to the expectations around us,' she wrote.[3]

But she did more than just talk about her values and views; she lived them. Prior to launching *Ms.*, she had co-founded the National Women's Political Caucus in 1971 along with more than three hundred other women. Still active today, the organization provides support and training for women candidates for elected and appointed offices. Later, she helped organize the 1977 National Women's Conference in Houston, Texas, USA, alongside Congresswoman Bella Abzug. The event garnered nationwide attention, with over 20,000 attendees discussing topics including foreign policy, education reform, and child care. And more importantly, it was significant in uniting women.

As her travels continued – both literal and figurative – she came to realize that her journey was far from over; perhaps it never would be. 'In my first days of activism, I thought I would do this ("this" being feminism) for a few years and then return to my real life,' she wrote in a piece for *Ms.* 'But like so many others now and in movements past, I've learned that this is not just something we care about for a year or two or three. We are in it for life – and for our lives. Not even the spiral of history is needed to show the distance travelled. We have only to look back at the less complete people we ourselves used to be.'[4]

Indeed, through the end of the twentieth century and into the twenty-first, Steinem's organizing lifestyle continued. In 1992 she co-founded Choice USA (now URGE: Unite for Reproductive & Gender Equity) to mobilize people in support of abortion rights, and has continued to be active in politics.

An itinerant organizer, Steinem, now age eighty-five, continues to travel and promote equality on the road. In *My Life on the Road* she encourages others to be open to the idea of a journey – long or short. But travel doesn't have to be the physical kind. It can be metaphorical, as in travelling into the history of a country, culture or person. Steinem has done both. One could say she is a nomadic soul, a wanderer. And her work is not done.

'A degree of honesty and authenticity is necessary for trust. Nothing works without trust.'

Prologue

We need to worry less about doing what is most important, and more about doing whatever we can. Those of us who are used to power need to learn to listen as much as we talk, and those with less power need to learn to talk as much as we listen. The truth is that we can't know which act in the present will make the most difference in the future, but we can behave as if everything we do matters.

Even the presence or absence of adjectives can challenge ranking. For instance, everybody except heterosexual white men still tends to require an adjective – as in women writers, black physicians and gay or lesbian candidates. The powerful only need the noun. Though we may still need adjectives to make 'out' groups visible, we can underline the politics of words by, say, using adjectives for the powerful, too. Thus, Philip Roth is not a novelist, but a man novelist, and Donald Trump is not a real estate developer but a white real estate developer. Since Hollywood belittles some movies about daily life as 'chick flicks,' why not call those about daily death 'prick flicks.'

Nothing is too small – or too big – to change consciousness.

All together, we are changing from a society whose organizing principle is the pyramid or hierarchy to one whose image is the circle. Humans are linked, not ranked. Humans and the environment are linked, not ranked.

And remember, the end doesn't justify the means; the means are the ends. If we want dancing and laughter and friendship and kindness in the future, we must have dancing and laughter and friendship and kindness along the way.

That is the small and the big of it.

At my age, in this still hierarchical time, people often ask me if I'm 'passing the torch.' I explain that I'm keeping my torch, thank you very much – and I'm using it to light the torches of others.

Because only if each of us has a torch will there be enough light.

From a talk at the National Press Club, Washington, D.C., USA, 19 November 2013, the night before Steinem received the Presidential Medal of Freedom

'We will not be quiet, we will not be controlled, we will work for a world in which all countries are connected. God may be in the details, but the goddess is in connections.'

The Interview

Apparently everything, this is the problem! But I think what's authentic, what's an emergency, or what is empathetic. In the end, what matters is what makes a personal connection to you, and also connects you to other people.

As a child, there was no social justice movement that I knew of. I knew that my mother cried when she heard President Roosevelt's name, because he had gotten us out of the depression, so I felt some connection to the government, I knew that was important. Other than that, I lived in books. Louisa May Alcott was my first friend. She was trying to be a writer, and wrote about the world of women, and the civil war.[i] So I would say my childhood was a combination of reading, and animals. I was completely bonkers about puppies and rabbits and horses. I think that's not uncommon in children, because you have that need for empathy, and yet you're too little . . . so [because] animals are littler than you, you can rescue them, and help them.

The real sensation of empathy is one from which, actually, I would exclude books. Because it turns out that we can only experience empathy when we're together with all five senses. We can learn, which is very important, but we can't know what someone else is feeling. We don't produce oxytocin, which is the hormone that literally allows us to connect with each other, and without which the species couldn't survive. I'm grateful that I had parents who I loved, and who loved me; and animals. And that I had fantasies for the future.

I would go to school until Halloween, and then it would get cold and my father would say, 'Okay, it's time to put everything in the house trailer, and go to Florida or California.' I didn't know any other way of life, except in the movies – which I kind of envied. I would see all of those kids with houses, and picket fences, and going to schools. But I was always sitting in the back of the car reading.

My mother would say, 'Look! Look what we're seeing.' And I would say, 'Oh, but I looked an hour ago.'

I only later in life grew to appreciate how important it was, in some ways, that I didn't go to school. Or that I'd only go for a couple of months. I didn't absorb racial difference that, probably, I otherwise would have. Or colouring in the lines. Of course, I can't do maths to this day, that's a problem. But I've grown to appreciate in later adult life a childhood that, at the time, I would have traded to be like everyone else.

*

As far as I know, every human being has the potential for empathy in varying degrees. If you give a baby to someone, male or female, they're flooded with empathy. If we see an accident, even if it's a stranger, we feel like we want to help because we're flooded with empathy. I do believe that we're all equipped with it to some degree. I think, probably, that females – and some other groups – can become empathy-sick, because you know what someone else is feeling, better than you know what you are feeling.

I often say to women, 'Look, the golden rule was great, written by a smart guy for guys. Do unto others as you would have done unto you.' But women probably need to reverse it. We need to learn to treat ourselves as well as we treat other people.

Has there been a special individual or individuals that have particularly inspired you by their example or wisdom?

I think of Wilma Mankiller, who was the chief of the Cherokee Nation here – our original nations before, unfortunately, Columbus showed up.[ii] The nations were very egalitarian, they were organized on a circle, not a pyramid. After a couple of centuries of bad times, she was the first elected female chief. She in herself was one hundred per cent authentic and funny and wise.

But she was also a link to the history we don't learn; which is before monotheism, before colonialism, before this 'country' only six hundred years ago, when there were all

these other cultures. Up till then I thought
that what I hoped for might exist in the future.
But then I discovered, 'Wait a minute, some
of this is memory. Some of this is maybe
in ourselves.' From the Khoisan in Africa,
from the Southern tip of India, from the old
cultures that – for, I think, political reasons –
we don't learn about. It's like there are two
things: history, and the past. And they are
not the same.

I became friends with Wilma because of
the Ms. Foundation for Women, which was
the first national women's foundation. We
started it because we wrongly thought that
Ms. Magazine was going to make a lot of
money – but of course we ended up having
to raise money. And we had native American
board members – I did not know Wilma,
but Rayna Green, who is also a Cherokee
anthropologist, recommended Wilma.[iii]

It was partly like meeting a tree –
because she's so rooted and natural – and
partly like meeting a great, mischievous
friend, because she was that too. I had only
begun to glimpse that, as they say, the root
of oppression is loss of memory. Wilma

really helped me see what had existed, and a little bit of what still exists, and then what could exist again.

It's kind of fundamental that we don't learn from sameness. We learn from difference. Always, what makes you curious, I think, is that this person represents something you don't know, and that that person is being honest. A degree of honesty and authenticity is necessary for trust. Nothing works without trust.

*

I have not had the experience of wanting to be exactly like someone else. I have had the experience of thinking, 'I want to do that, what they're doing.' I remember when I first moved to New York. I was walking on one of the main avenues here, and I looked across the street and I saw a woman in an Australian oil cloth raincoat, cowboy boots, cowboy hat, walking, no purse – somehow it was important to me that she didn't have a purse – and I only saw her for thirty seconds, and I thought, 'That is the first free woman I've ever seen in my life.

I want to be a free woman too.' And that was
a tiny, tiny moment. So I think the person
who's already in you seizes on things that are
going to help develop that unique person.

I do think that we're always trying to
express this unique person, and also to make
empathetic connections with others. I mean,
there's a reason why solitary confinement
is torture. We need to be together. But I
was profoundly lucky in the sense that my
parents were not monotheists of any kind.
My father had no interest in any kind of
religion or spirituality, but the women in the
family did. Because of who they were, they
recognized the individuality of each person,
and the human connectedness. So I didn't
have to – I wasn't born into a place where
I had to become just like Aunt Louise, or
some other person.

'One of the simplest paths to deep change is for the less powerful to speak as much as they listen, and for the more powerful to listen as much as they speak.'

Do you have guiding principles or a driving
philosophy that underpins your life and decisions?

I do, because I understand that instant
democracy comes from talking as much as
you listen, and listening as much as you talk;
if you just equalize those things that's kind of
an instant democracy right there. Since the
ends are the means, that's really the only way
you can continue to create democracy. I do
realize that now.

But I think a lot of it is beyond rational
process, because – and this is my favourite
instinct story – if it walks like a duck, and
looks like a duck, and quacks like a duck, and
you think it's a pig, it's a pig. I think you know
when somebody is authentic in themselves,
or being honest, or knows something you
don't know, and therefore curiosity – which is
such a wonderful, wonderful force on earth –
it's present, and it's in the moment.

*

We are just literally, factually, a combination
of heredity and environment in a unique way,

that could never have happened before, and could never happen again. And we share all of humanity. I think we are both trying to become who we already are, and we very much need people who respect difference; who don't expect sameness, who see each person as unique. I was lucky, in the sense that my mother and both of my grandmothers, were theosophists, so they kind of believed in reincarnation.

The theosophical idea of childrearing is that your duty as parents and family is to love and care for that child. And help that child become who they already are. This is a great philosophy, because it means you don't have to just be like Uncle Harry, or the whole family. I was lucky in that way.

You have talked about listening, and about talking circles – what have talking circles meant to you, and why are they so important?

First of all, there is no straight line in nature, so the very idea that we have boundaries between countries, or that we have theatres with rows, or we have divisions like this, is completely artificial. And if you were in Africa, say, and you're going from a city into the bush, you can see the lines disappear. Even ploughing is done circularly around, and if we ploughed that way here, we wouldn't have erosion like we do. The circle, or the curve, is the natural, natural form. So I find just sitting in a circle, that already makes a difference. And if, from the beginning, each person's voice is heard – if you go around at least once so everyone speaks, no matter what you say – it makes you into a group.

Just the simple idea of both listening and talking, of being part of it, literally makes you into a group. That is almost as important as air and water. Now, for instance, because in this country and many others, people are spending so much time looking at screens, phones and computers – I believe it's now ten or eleven hours a day here – from that time in the late eighties forward, loneliness, depression, suicide, has greatly increased. We are meant to be communal animals. We are meant to be together. We're trying to recreate that to get out of hierarchies, to get out of isolation in front of our screens.

It's important, it's a great learning. But we have to spend an hour with other people for every hour we spend looking at a screen.

As someone who's fought for change, has listening been a powerful tool in your armoury?

In the beginning, we kind of choose our profession for a reason. I had been two things in my life, a dancer and a writer. And both of them meant I didn't want to talk. When I had to begin to speak, because there was no other way of communicating what was happening in the movement, I went to a speech teacher. And she said, 'Well of course my dear, you've chosen those things because you don't want to talk.' So I began to leave half the time to talk with the audience, partly because I literally didn't want to talk all the time.

But in that way, I discovered how much more fun and exciting, and filled with learning it is. And to this day, really, I have to fight with people. If I'm going to do a lecture, they will say, 'Well, we have to write the questions on cards even before you speak; but they won't know what you'll be saying.

Because otherwise someone else will get up and take over the floor.' And I always said, 'Listen, if somebody gets up and talks too long, someone else will tell them to sit down.' You have to trust the audience, to just let it happen. It works in different ways, but it never fails to work.

What qualities have been most critical to achieving goals during your life and career?

I would say that the single most important thing is that I lucked into was, as a writer, often being able to write about what I cared about. But because I am fortunate enough to be alive in a time of social justice movements – a movement just means you have friends who are doing the same thing, that's what a movement is – I've been lucky to be alive at the right time. And it's a gift in every possible way. It's a gift because you do learn from difference, and there's plenty of it. It's a gift because it's also multi-generational.

I think age is as terrible as any other kind of segregation. We need to organize, or be together; if you're old you have hope, because you remember when it was worse. And if you're young, you're mad as hell because it should be better. So we need both those things. We can instruct each other.

*

I grew up reading, and loving individual writers – so I always wanted to be a writer. I was trying to write about what I was curious about, or what I thought wasn't well known enough. So it just seemed a natural progression. I was lucky enough to be able to continue in that way, and to become someone who has never actually had a job. I've always been freelancing. And of course part of that is that I don't have children to support, I only have to support myself. And I was accustomed to living a peripatetic life because I grew up that way.

'Movements are like rivers.
Dipping into them is never
the same twice.'

Do you think 'truth talking' is an important quality?

Yes, it is. Because I feel that when I read Alice Walker,[iv] or Robin Morgan, you know you're not alone, they're there carrying your thoughts further. Sometimes, in very few words, Robin Morgan says, 'Hate generalizes, love specifies.' That's pretty good for four words, right? It's following interest and curiosity, and the "aha" factor.[v]

And I have to say something else: following laughter. Laughter is an absolute clue to freedom. Laughter is the only emotion you can't compel. Fear, we know. But even love, if you're dependent for long enough, you become enmeshed. It's like the Stockholm Syndrome, you think you're attached to that person. But laughter only happens when you understand something, see two things come together.

And the original cultures here, and I'm sure on other continents too, recognize that. They have personified laughter as various, neither male nor female, spirits. Laughter breaks into the unknown, they say. If you can't laugh, you can't pray. I think what is most precious is not the deliberative, saying, 'I'm going to do this' . . . But when things come together, and you have a realisation, and you know it's right.

In a very profound way, I've learned that money is boring. Okay, we all need enough to eat, and a nice place to live, and going dancing, but we're made to think that rich people – just because they're rich – are interesting. So not true! And women get to realize this especially, because if you're growing up with a man who is accepted in that world, you're accepted too. And so you can see how boring it is.

If someone comes up to me and tells me that something I've been a part of has been helpful in their lives, and they tell me what happened, that is so much more rewarding than just adding up dollars, it's incredible. I want to go give a course at Harvard Business School called "Money Is Boring", and a little sub-seminar called "How Much Is Enough?"

Because I think we're just made to feel that accumulating is great. And also, inheritance I think is a problem, because it destroys people. I am so grateful I didn't inherit money.

I think we're all worrying understandably if it's about food and shelter, and your kids and their education. That makes perfect sense. But beyond that, it just doesn't have meaning. Now, we have to worry about it, especially because we're in a time of such economic division. It's actually, I think, worse than the Depression now, because there's huge accumulated wealth among very few people. People say, 'Oh, your unemployment rate is low in this country.' Yes, the reason it's low is because many people have to work two jobs, because otherwise they can't make a living.

Can you describe a key moment or crisis which has particularly tested you?

I think the most difficult crisis is when people with whom you agree, and with whom you're working, for various other reasons disapprove of you. There are a lot of people who, if they approved of me, I'd be terrified! 'What am

I doing wrong!' But when it's our colleagues and compatriots – people who for all kinds of reasons have not been able to realize themselves – when they see someone else doing it, it's called the 'crabs in the basket syndrome' here. I think it's also called the 'tall poppy syndrome'. Everybody's trying to get out of the basket, and we'll pull down the one who's getting up instead of using that as a chain to get up. I think that's been the most painful thing.

How do you deal with mistakes you've made or endeavours that have failed?

I find it hard to get over the habit of second-guessing myself, and especially because I was not a natural public speaker. Even now I only worry about two things – what I did say, and what I didn't say. And you kind of go around rehearsing. I find it hard to get over that. Mostly, I would say the habit of mine that probably is not good, is that I live in the future. I'm always saying to myself, 'Well, what if we did *that*, maybe *that* would happen?'

And since you can't live fully in the future – you only can live in the present – it's something that I'm always worried about. I'm a little worried that I'm going to die saying, 'But!'

What does leadership mean to you?

Leadership mainly means "by example". I think we do what we see, way, way more than what we're told. So when we see somebody who is achieving or realizing something that we also want to achieve or realize – and especially if we can relate to that person; it's not that women can only relate to women, or black people [can only relate to black people], but if everybody doesn't look like you, it's difficult – you need to know that there are *some* other people who look like you, who have accomplished what you want to accomplish.

Wilma Mankiller comes to mind. Her magic was just her presence, she's very authentic. And very – from serious to laughter – all-present. Very honest.

Alice Walker, who leads by her writing and by her life example.

I would say that Gandhi comes to mind,
except that, of course, from living in India
I realized that he was actually copying the
women's movement in his organizing tactics,
which I didn't know until much later. I went
to talk to a woman named Kamaladevi
Chattopadhyay, who's very famous, a
wonderful woman who worked with Gandhi.[vi]

With a friend, we were going to write a
little booklet about Gandhian tactics, because
we thought it would be helpful to women's
groups around the world. And she listened
to us very patiently, and then she said,
'Well my dear, we taught him everything.'
I think that's interesting too, because
sometimes, – I think it was Vita Sackville-
West[vii] who said, 'I worshipped dead men
for their strength, forgetting I was strong.' –
sometimes we're attracted to something
in someone else that, actually, is in us.

*

I think there's something else which – as
I began to realize what we don't learn in
school, or maybe we're just beginning to

learn – is that the cultures, the five hundred
or so different languages and cultures that
were here in North America before Europeans
showed up, were actually superior in terms
of medicine and growing techniques, politics.
We copied our Constitution from the Iroquois
Confederacy. It's the oldest, continuous
democracy in the world. So here were all
these enormously sophisticated cultures, and
suddenly this influx of European, English,
colonial – plus disease, which people here
were not immune to.

And just the generations and generations
of decimation, physical decimation, and doing
away with history, and taking generations
upon generations of kids and forbidding them
to speak their own language. And sending
them to terrible boarding schools where
they were sexually abused. Just horrendous,
horrendous. I would always say to Wilma
[Mankiller], and Rebecca Adamson,[viii] and
other women who are from these cultures –
and some men too – 'How can you bear it?
How can you bear it?' And they always say,
'We're still here'.

We can't 100 per cent judge why, but we know how. The 'why' may be that there was a kind of a great disaster, a meteor passing close, so all the legends of floods and so on are probably not wrong, so the older cultures in Europe got wiped out. Also using the horse was discovered at the same time, which was like the atom bomb of the era because you could travel more quickly. Europe seems to have become patriarchal, which just means controlling women as the means of reproduction.

First, it got profoundly overpopulated, and it invented racism to justify taking over other people's countries – to say, 'These people are inferior, so it's okay we're killing them.' King Leopold, you know, killed half the people.[ix] And monotheism, because the idea, the original and continuing idea of spirituality is [that] there's godliness in all living things. Monotheism makes God look like the ruling class, and if you make the trip on the Nile, you go from the Nubian, older African parts towards Cairo, you can see it in the ancient carvings. You can see that in the oldest parts of the Nile, everything is represented.

Snakes and butterflies, and papyrus, men and women, everything.

And then a thousand years later there's not so much nature – the goddess has a son and no daughter. Then a thousand years later there's even less. The son has grown up to be a god, and the goddess his throne. You can just see it happening. And at the time I was reading Henry Breasted, who's an Egyptologist, and he said, 'The withdrawal of God from women and nature was to make it okay to conquer women and nature.'[x]

So I do think that monotheism is *way* part of the problem, not the solution, and part of the reason [for] colonialism was the Bible and the sword. It was trying to seize control of people's minds, as well as their bodies. I'm not trying to say that many people haven't found community, and found truth and helpfulness in a religion. But the very idea that God is of one gender, or one race. I mean, why is Jesus blonde-haired and blue-eyed in the middle of the Middle East? It's very suspicious.

'In truth, we don't know which of our acts in the present will shape the future. But we have to behave as if everything we do matters. Because it might.'

What do you think the world needs more of?

I'm torn between two things: saying that
we need to meet with all five senses more,
on the one hand, and saying we need a
big fact-checking service, on the other. The
combination of the internet and advertising –
because advertising doesn't reward accuracy,
it rewards number of eyeballs – if it weren't
for advertising, we wouldn't have Donald
Trump. I mean, he lost the election anyway by
six million votes, so we have to get rid of the
Electoral College, which only the slave states
wanted in the first place.

But no one would know who he is if he
had not been in this godawful television show,
which became popular because it was like
watching a roadside accident. Actually, one
of the people responsible for it said, 'Donald
Trump may not be good for the country, but
he's good for CBS.' I would say we need a
huge fact-checking service, and we need
to pay for our own media, instead of letting
advertising pay for it all.

Trump is a prime example of narcissistic
personality disorder. You can predict everything

he's going to do, because he will respond with extreme hostility to the smallest criticism. And he will slavishly follow any praise. You get those two things, and you can predict everything he does. But he's not a sane person. When asked why voters did vote for him, the most frequent reason was that he was a good businessman. He's a terrible businessman. If he had just invested the money he had inherited he'd be much richer than he is now.

*

I think it's important to understand that we are each unique, and also share our humanity. And that the family is the root of everything. If there is violence in the family, it's going to normalize violence, it's going to be difficult to uproot violence after that. If there's a hierarchy in the family which says that men don't do the dishes, or worse, there's violence – that is reflected everywhere else.

The one virtue of computers is that now we can prove this, we can show that the single biggest determinant of whether a country will be violent inside itself, in its streets, or will be willing to use military violence against another country – it's not poverty, not access to natural resources, not degree of democracy even, or religion; it's violence against females. Not because female life is any more important than male life, it's not. But because of patriarchy and controlling reproduction, and controlling the one thing men don't have – which is wombs.

Half the human race can only control the other half with violence, or the threat of violence. So if you see that in your household, you come to believe it's inevitable that one group is meant to dominate another. And we can see it all around us, even though it's not spoken of in our news programmes. If you look at terrorist groups, you'll find they are extremely gender-polarized. Extremely polarized. If you look at peaceful, or more democratic groups, they're way less polarized. If we can learn that, I think it also empowers us, because we know that the way that we live every day, the families we have, how we educate our kids, how we receive this unique person, and make sure we listen to that person, not just tell them what to do – that is the root of a larger, post-democratic and more peaceful possibility.

What advice would you give your twenty-year-old self?

That's so hard, because I don't know she'd listen! I guess I would just say: One, it's going to be alright; and two, you can't possibly predict what's going to happen, so just enjoy it as it comes.

A final thought

How gender is made up, and how race is made up, is so pervasive in this country, still. And I think the fear of refugees is all based on that difference.

If there were a requirement that there were fifty-fifty, women and men in leadership roles, it might be better, but it would depend how they were picked. For instance, at the Indian village level, the governing system, they tried to do that. And there are all kinds of cartoons – the men are sitting at the table, the women aren't, because they just brought their wives who couldn't even talk.

It depends if the women can self-select, that they aren't just echoes of who is already there. It's not as if our brains are determined by our genitals, no. Both men and women can be universal people. But women do have a whole set of experiences, and are brought up without dominance as a goal, or hierarchy as such a goal. I mean our model is more likely to be nurturing, or the family, and that's very helpful.

'Change does come from the bottom up, and it will come from girls and women and men who understand that for us all to be human beings instead of being grouped by gender is good for them, too.'

'There are no *should's*. You do everything you can: How you spend your money, how you vote, the kind of language you use, you name unfairness when you see it – every day presents all these opportunities. The danger comes from looking up there and asking, "What should I do?" instead of looking at each other and saying, "I'm going to do everything I can."'

About Gloria Steinem

Gloria Steinem is an American writer, lecturer, feminist organizer and frequent media commentator on issues of equality and gender. She was born in Toledo, Ohio, USA, on 25 March 1934. After studying at Smith College she spent two years in India on a fellowship, writing for Indian publications, and went on to establish herself as a freelance writer, gaining attention for her 1963 expose for *Show* magazine, where she went undercover as a Playboy Bunny at New York's Playboy Club.

In 1968 Steinem co-founded *New York* magazine, for which she wrote a political column and feature articles, and in 1972 she co-founded pioneering feminist magazine *Ms. Magazine*, for which she remains a consulting editor. Her writing has appeared in essays and articles for major US and international publications, including the *New York Times Magazine*, *Cosmopolitan*, *The Guardian* and *Esquire*. Her journalistic career has earned her a multitude of awards, including the Penney-Missouri Journalism Award, the Women's Sports Journalism Award, the Lifetime Achievement in Journalism Award from the Society of Professional Journalists, the Society of Writers Award from the United Nations, the James Weldon Johnson Medal for Journalism, and the 2015 Richard C. Holbrooke Distinguished Achievement Award.

Steinem helped found various organizations focussed on generating equal rights for women across the board, including the Women's Action Alliance, the National Women's Political Caucus, the Women's Media Center and the Ms. Foundation for Women and its initiative, Take Our Daughters to Work Day. She is openly pro-choice and co-founded political action committee Voters for Choice, and the national organization Choice USA (now URGE), which supports young pro-choice leadership. She was a member of the Beyond Racism Initiative, a joint initiative between South Africa, Brazil and the US, and helped found Equality Now, Donor Direct Action, and Direct Impact Africa.

Steinem has written a number of books, including *Revolution from Within*, *Moving Beyond Words*, *Outrageous Acts and Everyday Rebellions*, and the *New York Times* bestselling *My Life on the Road*. She has produced films and documentaries focussed on social and political issues including violence against women, child abuse, and capital punishment, and has been the subject of three television documentaries.

Steinem has received numerous honours, including the United Nation's Ceres Medal, the Presidential Medal of Freedom, a Doctorate of Human Justice, and the American Civil Liberties Union of Southern California's Bill of Rights Awards. She lives and works in New York City, USA.

gloriasteinem.com

About the Project

'A true leader must work hard
to ease tensions, especially
when dealing with sensitive and
complicated issues. Extremists
normally thrive when there is
tension, and pure emotion tends
to supersede rational thinking.'

– Nelson Mandela

Inspired by Nelson Mandela, *I Know This to Be True* was
conceived to record and share what really matters for the
most inspiring leaders of our time.

I Know This to Be True is a Nelson Mandela Foundation
project anchored by original interviews with twelve
different and extraordinary leaders each year, for five
years – six men and six women – who are helping and
inspiring others through their ideas, values and work.

Royalties from sales of this book will support language
translation and free access to films, books and educational
programmes using material from the series, in all countries
with developing economies, or economies in transition,
as defined by United Nations annual classifications.

iknowthistobetrue.org

The People Behind the Project

'A good head and a good
heart are always a formidable
combination.'

– Nelson Mandela

A special thanks to Gloria Steinem, and all the generous and inspiring individuals we call leaders who have magnanimously given their time to be part of this project.

For the Nelson Mandela Foundation:
Sello Hatang, Verne Harris, Noreen Wahome, Razia Saleh and Sahm Venter

For Blackwell & Ruth:
Geoff Blackwell, Ruth Hobday, Cameron Gibb, Nikki Addison, Olivia van Velthooven, Elizabeth Blackwell, Kate Raven, Annie Cai and Tony Coombe

We hope that together we can help to mobilize Madiba's extraordinary legacy, to the benefit of communities around the world.

A note from the photographer

The photographic portraits in this book are the result of a team effort, led by Blackwell & Ruth's talented design director Cameron Gibb, who both mentored and saved this fledgling photographer. I have long harboured the desire, perhaps conceit, that I could personally create photographs for one of our projects, but through many trials, and more than a few errors, I learned that without Cameron's generous direction and sensitivity, I couldn't have come close to creating these portraits.

– Geoff Blackwell

About Nelson Mandela

Nelson Mandela was born in the Transkei, South Africa, on 18 July 1918. He joined the African National Congress in the early 1940s and was engaged in struggles against the ruling National Party's apartheid system for many years before being arrested in August 1962. Mandela was incarcerated for more than twenty-seven years, during which his reputation as a potent symbol of resistance for the anti-apartheid movement grew steadily. Released from prison in 1990, Mandela was jointly awarded the Nobel Peace Prize in 1993, and became South Africa's first democratically elected president in 1994. He died on 5 December 2013, at the age of ninety-five.

NELSON MANDELA
FOUNDATION
Living the legacy

About the Nelson Mandela Foundation

The Nelson Mandela Foundation is a non-profit organization founded by Nelson Mandela in 1999 as his post-presidential office. In 2007 he gave it a mandate to promote social justice through dialogue and memory work.

Its mission is to contribute to the making of a just society by mobilizing the legacy of Nelson Mandela, providing public access to information on his life and times and convening dialogue on critical social issues.

The Foundation strives to weave leadership development into all aspects of its work.

nelsonmandela.org

Notes

i   Louisa May Alcott (1832–88), American novelist, author of
     Little Women.

ii   Wilma Pearl Mankiller (1945–2010), Cherokee activist and social
     worker, first woman elected to serve as Principal Chief of the
     Cherokee Nation.

iii Rayna Diane Green (b. 1942), author and anthropologist. Curator
     and director of the American Indian Program at the National
     Museum of American History at the Smithsonian Institution,
     Washington, D.C., USA.

iv   Alice Walker (b. 1944), American, feminist, and social activist.
     Author of *The Color Purple* which was awarded the National
     Book Award and the Pulitzer Prize.

v   Robin Morgan (b. 1941), American poet, author, and activist.
     Editor of *Ms. Magazine*.

vi   Kamaladevi Chattopadhya (1903–88), Indian social activist
     and feminist, active in the Indian Independence movement.

vii Vita Sackville-West (1892–1962), English poet and novelist,
     author of *Portrait of a Marriage*.

viii Rebecca Adamson (b. 1950), Cherokee advocate. Founder of First
     Nations Development Institute, and of First Peoples Worldwide.

ix   Leopold II of Belgium (1835—1909). Founder of the Congo
     Free State in 1885, now the Democratic Republic of the Congo.
     Responsible for widespread torture, atrocities and murder
     committed against the Congolese people during his rule,
     with estimates of between one and fifteen million deaths.

x   James Henry Breasted (1865–1935), American archaeologist,
     Egyptologist, and historian.

Sources and Permissions

1   Gloria Steinem, *My Life on the Road* (Random House, an imprint
      and division of Penguin Random House LLC, New York, USA, 2015),
      p. xix.

2   GS, "Op-ed: On Working Together Over Time", *Advocate*,
      2 October 2013.

3   GS, *My Life on the Road* (Random House, an imprint and division
      of Penguin Random House LLC, New York, USA, 2015), p. 39.

4   GS, "Far From the Opposite Shore: How to Survive Though a
      Feminist", *Ms. Magazine*, July 1978, p. 65.

The publisher is grateful for literary permissions to reproduce items
subject to copyright which have been used with permission. Every effort
has been made to trace the copyright holders and the publisher apologizes
for any unintentional omission. We would be pleased to hear from any
not acknowledged here and undertake to make all reasonable efforts to
include the appropriate acknowledgement in any subsequent edition.

Pages 6, 11, 14, 35, 53: *My Life on the Road* by Gloria Steinem, copyright
© 2015 by Gloria Steinem, used by permission of Random House, an
imprint and division of Penguin Random House LLC, all rights reserved,
and reproduced with permission of the Licensor through PLSclear; pages
11, 42: "Op-ed: On Working Together Over Time", Gloria Steinem, *Advocate*,
2 October 2013, advocate.com/commentary/2013/10/02/op-ed-working-
together-over-time; page 15: "Far From the Opposite Shore: How to Survive
Though a Feminist", Gloria Steinem, *Ms. Magazine*, July 1978, issue no.
65; pages 19–20: a talk given by Gloria Steinem at the National Press Club
in Washington, D.C., USA, on 19 November 2013. Full text appears in the
Winter/Spring 2014 issue of *Ms. Magazine*, msmagazine.com/2015/03/21/
our-revolution-has-just-begun; page 21: Gloria Steinem 2017 Women's March
speech, Washington, D.C., USA, 21 January, 2017; page 59: "Interview
with Gloria Steinem on Equality, Her New Memoir and More", Marianne
Schnall, Feminist.com, feminist.com/resources/artspeech/interviews/
gloriasteineminterview; page 62: "Gloria Steinem's Advice for the Next
Generation of Feminists is a Must-Read for Our Time", Mary Wang, *Vogue*,
14 October 2017, copyright © Conde Nast; pages 69–70: *Nelson Mandela
by Himself: The Authorised Book of Quotations* edited by Sello Hatang and
Sahm Venter (Pan Macmillan: Johannesburg, South Africa, 2017), copyright
© 2011 Nelson R. Mandela and the Nelson Mandela Foundation, used by
permission of the Nelson Mandela Foundation, Johannesburg, South Africa.

First published in the United States of America in 2020 by Chronicle Books LLC.

Produced and originated by
Blackwell and Ruth Limited
Suite 405, Ironbank,150 Karangahape Road
Auckland 1010, New Zealand
www.blackwellandruth.com

Publisher: Geoff Blackwell
Editor in Chief & Project Editor: Ruth Hobday
Design Director: Cameron Gibb
Designer & Production Coordinator: Olivia van Velthooven
Publishing Manager: Nikki Addison
Digital Publishing Manager: Elizabeth Blackwell

Library of Congress Cataloging-in-Publication Data available.

ISBN 978-1-7972-0018-7

Chronicle Books LLC
680 Second Street
San Francisco, CA 94107
www.chroniclebooks.com

10 9 8 7 6 5 4 3 2 1

Manufactured in China by 1010 Printing Ltd.

Also available in the series:
Stephen Curry: on family, determination & passion
Ruth Bader Ginsburg: on equality, determination & service
Bryan Stevenson: on equality, justice & compassion
Greta Thunberg: on truth, courage & saving our planet
Nelson Mandela: guiding principles by Sello Hatang & Verne Harris